Relax & Write

Relax & Write

tapping your unconscious
for life and art

Maia Danziger

Library of Congress Cataloging-in-Publication Data

Danziger, Maia, 1950-
 Relax & write : tapping your unconscious for life and art / Maia Danziger.
  p. cm.
 ISBN-13: 978-0-557-56330-2 (pbk.)
 1. Subconsciousness. 2. Relaxation. 3. Self-help techniques. 4. Authorship—
Psychological aspects. 5. Creation (literary, artistic, etc.)—Psychological aspects.
I. Title. II. Title: Relax and write.
 BF315.D36 2006
 154.2—dc22

                                        2006025758

Printed in USA

To Kit, for his unwavering support and love.

And to Dustin and Toby, who taught me how to love and grow.

FOR MP3 DOWNLOAD:

go to: relaxandwrite.com

password: relaxandwrite

table of contents

acknowledgments

The seeds of *Relax & Write* were sown in Manhattan with my fellow travelers Wendy Bichel, Martha Davis, Alethea Worden, and Tara Lane.

Endless gratitude to my teaching mentors: Jill Purce, who opened my spirit, and Larry Moss, who taught me the healing power of the creative process, and who continues to call me forth into places I think I can't go.

Thanks to Betsy Amster, who believed in the book and helped me to find my author's voice.

To Andrea Richards for her friendship and enthusiasm, and to Amy Inouye for her sensibility and exquisite eye.

And, of course, to my students, without whom none of this would be possible.

introduction

O n opening night of my first professional
show, I stood backstage at the Circle in the
Square Theatre on Broadway and peered out
from the wings at the gathering crowd. I was very young
and very frightened. As the house lights dimmed, I felt a
hand on my shoulder. "Are you scared, kid?" I looked up
into Eli Wallach's eyes. I nodded. "Terrified." "Don't be,"
he said. "You've done your work. Now just relax and stay
out of your own way."

"Just relax." It seemed so simple and yet impos-
sible at the time—if stage fright didn't get to me, all
my notions about "gearing up" for a performance surely
would. Wasn't I supposed to be running on nerves? Isn't
that what made a performance "electric?" The stage
lights came up and Mr. Wallach, with a deep breath and
a fatherly wink, sailed onstage.

Over the years I have come to regard that ex-
change as one of the most profound lessons in creativity—and life—I've ever had. Relax and stay out of your
own way. But how? We all know that the path to creativity is lined with obstacles (think of all those stories about
the oyster needing a grain of sand to create a pearl). But

what if it were possible to meet those obstacles not with resistance and strain but with curiosity?

When I began graduate studies in creative writing at NYU, after years of performing on and off-Broadway, my old stage fright translated into anxiety whenever I faced the dreaded blank page. I longed to be able to drop into my characters' thoughts and lives as easily as I inhabited a role onstage. Often I would light a candle before sitting down to write, hoping to still myself enough to let my inner voice be heard. "Just relax and stay out of your own way." Easy to say. But it wasn't always so easy to do. Mostly it was hit-or-miss, the muse was with me or not. I had no way to find her on my own.

As an actress I had studied deep breathing techniques, yoga, Qigong, and meditation as ways to bypass my fight-or-flight impulse before an audition and stay open to my instincts in the moment. When I combined this with "sense memory" (one of the foundations of Method acting, which teaches you to concentrate on a sensory experience for emotional recall), my focus and awareness seemed to increase; by giving my very active conscious mind something specific to do, my unconscious and creative impulses were let out to play. It made sense that these techniques should apply to my writing.

I began to approach my creative life as a spiritual practice, a meditative discipline that could expand my awareness and bring me closer to my inner voice. It worked. When I created a safe and open space within, my "muse" appeared to fill it. Like the magical child the imagination is, all it asked for was to be welcomed home.

These days, when I teach my *Relax & Write* work-

shops, I am always amazed at how few of us are trained to slow down and listen when we sit down to write. Our minds are so filled with what we "should" write, what we think we want to write, or the fear that we haven't got anything at all to write, that we forget to check in with the only place that matters—our inner selves. This is where our stories live and where our true voice can be heard. There's a feeling that accessing this inner material is something miraculous, that it happens by chance or luck. This belief is as strongly held by seasoned writers as it is by novices. But it's not true. Every one of us has lived great stories and has a voice to tell them with—the only thing some of us are lacking, as the Wizard said to Dorothy, is the means of transportation.

The process outlined in *Relax & Write* is a kind of hot-air balloon to creative Oz. It's nearly as simple as clicking ruby slippers together: relax, follow the journey, travel to your own unconscious. Does it happen the first time out? More often than not, yes, and with practice it is as reliable as Auntie Em.

Here's how to use this book: turn off your phones and pager, find a quiet, comfortable place alone or with friends. Take off your shoes, lower the lights, light a candle if you like. This is about leaving all the stress behind. If leaving stress behind feels stressful, take it slowly. This is a practice; you'll get used to it over time.

The starting point for each journey is the Deep Relaxation exercise. You'll do this every time you sit down to write. Get to know it. It's your friend. It will bring your awareness away from the distractions of the

outside world and toward your vast inner resources. From this place of relaxation, you will move into the guided meditation. Each meditation travels a suggested route—to a childhood home, a fork in the road, something you've lost or someone you need to find, to name a few. The journey is meant as a guidepost for your inner experience, a path to follow. But if you discover that your imagination is off and running (if, for example, the meditation says you are walking down the path, but in your mind's eye you're flying), follow your own experience. There are no right or wrong ways to do this work.

At the end of each journey you will begin to write. Set an alarm. You'll write for a minimum of thirty minutes. Write whatever comes up. Describe your journey. Describe anything else that's happening. If you're feeling resistance, write your resistance ("This feels uncomfortable. My neck aches. I'm hungry"). Above all, just keep writing. When the alarm goes off, stop writing. Take a break. Have some cookies. You've worked hard.

The next step is really important: read what you've written aloud. You don't know what you've written until you hear it, and reading it aloud often allows for an unexpected emotional resonance.

It is my belief that all good creative (and personal) work comes from a place of safety. In order to feel free enough to access all your material, you have to know that you're in control. To that end, the first journey in this book (and in every class I teach) is "A Safe Place." It is a profound experience to locate a place of safety within, and for many people this journey is destination enough— but for travelers on the *Relax & Write* path, it's only the

beginning. The unconscious is a vast and, for the most part, uncharted territory. I hope this book will serve as a field guide, a trusted source for journeying safely to your most important destination—your creative self.

DEEP RELAXATION EXERCISE
(Use this before every meditation.)

Begin seated in a chair, your feet resting comfort-
ably on the ground. Take a few deep breaths.
Don't force them. Just breathe in deeply, and
slowly and gently let the breath out. As you
breathe, notice that you are sitting on a chair.
Notice what parts of your body are touching the
chair. How the backs of your legs rest against the
seat. Does your back touch the back of the chair?
Maybe it does, maybe it doesn't. Just notice. Notice what your arms are doing. Are they lying in
your lap? Are they on the arms of the chair? Are
they at your side? Notice how your feet touch the
ground. Is your weight solidly over both feet, or
off to one side? Be aware that at this moment you
are completely supported. The chair is supporting the weight of your body, the ground beneath
you is supporting your feet. There is no need for
you to hold yourself up at all. You don't have to
do anything. Notice how that makes you feel. Is
there any place that might still be holding on? Are
you making yourself sit up in the chair? Just notice, and then let it go. Are you holding your legs
under you? Let them go, let the ground beneath

you take that weight. Now think down to your feet. Feel them solidly on the ground. Feel how the weight of gravity pulls them down, and for just a moment, imagine that force of gravity pulling down from somewhere underneath your feet. Picture that magnetic force making your legs feel heavy. Feel it pulling your soles, your toes, your arches. Just give over to that force of gravity, and let it all become heavy. Feel the heaviness of your ankles. Feel the heaviness move up into your shins and your calves. Don't resist, just let it all go. Feel how heavy your knees are, your thighs, the backs of your hips, your lower back, your buttocks, just feel that force of gravity pulling from the center of the earth. Give into it. Let everything go. Your torso, your rib cage, your mid-back, just let it go, your chest, your shoulders, the tops of your arms, your elbows, forearms, wrists, hands. Everything heavy. Gently shake your hands for a moment and feel how heavy they are. Give into that force of gravity that's pulling from the center of the earth. Let your palms be heavy, your fingers. Now move to your neck, your throat. There's no need to hold anything up, just give over to that force of gravity. Let your jaw be heavy, let it drop open, let your mouth hang open, no tension, no strain. The back of your jaw, the back of

your throat, the back of your tongue, just let it all drop and be heavy. The roof of your mouth, your teeth, inside your nose, your sinuses, just feel the weight of gravity, let everything be heavy. Your cheeks, your eyelids, your scalp, the back of your head, give everything over to the force of gravity and the support of your chair. You are completely and totally supported.

JOURNEY 1

a safe place

Frodo was now safe in the Last Homely House east of the Sea. That house was, as Bilbo had long ago reported, "a perfect house, whether you like food or sleep or storytelling or singing, or just sitting and thinking best, or a pleasant mixture of them all." Merely to be there was a cure for weariness, fear and sadness.

—J.R.R. Tolkien, The Fellowship of the Ring

On a brilliant late afternoon in February of 1994, the world as I knew it came to an end. I had squeezed my yearly mammogram in between appointments and was hastily buttoning my blouse in the exam room, when the technician came in. "The doctor would like another picture of your right breast," she said. I pulled my sweater over my head. "Sorry," I said. "I've gotta go. I haven't got time." She was young, so the authority of her voice caught me short. "Yes, you do," she answered. "Believe me, you've got time." When I stumbled out of the office an hour or so later, I had crossed the threshold into an alternate universe where the soothing comfort of my daily routine no longer counted. I had become a cancer patient. A person who might die before my time. A citizen of an unsafe world.

Of course, we are all citizens of an unsafe world. We have only to turn on the news to be reminded that life is fragile. The truth is, none of us gets out alive. So while the line I crossed that day from working actress, wife, stepmother of two teenagers, and artistic director of a theatre company to mere mortal seemed enormous, I was really only dropping into the truth of my own existence. In the face of that truth, every pore of my being yearned to find a safe space that I imagined existed somewhere just beyond my reach. I wanted to be held and rocked, wanted someone to kiss my fear away, to tell me that the monster wasn't hiding under my bed. But the monster was there, and no amount of wishing would change that reality. It was up to me to find a way to wake up every day and show up for my life. To make myself feel safe.

Over the course of the next several years, through surgeries and chemotherapy, the end of my marriage, the death of my mother and even my dog, I developed some clear notions of what I needed to do to hold my own equilibrium. I learned that often I felt most safe alone in a crowd; sitting in coffee shops observing everyday life gave me a sense of connection. Lighting candles in a darkened room or sitting quietly with my eyes closed seemed to still my anxiety when I felt overwhelmed. A hot bubble bath, a Fred Astaire and Ginger Rogers movie, old Warner Brothers cartoons—all became my best friends when the news from the outside world was hard. Like a magician, I filled my bag full of tricks to fool my frightened mind—sleight-of-hand for my soul. Most of the time it worked.

Knowing what makes you feel safe—whether it's the dream of something you longed for and never had, or whether it exists somewhere in your daily life—makes the resource more available. It's like hunting for buried treasure: if you've got the map, it doesn't take long. Sometimes when I find myself needing comfort, all I have to do is imagine a bubble bath, feel the water on my skin, smell the herbal scent, recall the steam rising up to my face and before I know it, I'm at peace.

Here's what I know about safety: we all long for it. Whatever our race or religion, even our species, it is a central organizing principle of all living creatures to find a safe space. Watch the lengths turtles go to when laying their eggs, the territorial instinct of animals in the wild, the borders and boundaries we humans erect in an attempt to assure the safety of ourselves and our kind. When the ground beneath our feet begins to shift, we scramble for a sense of balance. But the outside world is always shifting, and, more often than not, we have little control over its direction. If we're going to find any sense of safety—any North Star to steer by—we're going to have to find it deep inside ourselves.

In this exercise, you will journey to your own safe place. Maybe it's a place from your childhood (or maybe not), maybe it's a room or a chair or a grassy knoll under a tree. Maybe it's a place that exists, or some place you've only imagined. Maybe it's somewhere you've never dreamed of. Stay open and curious—go with what comes and figure it out later. After all, it's all in your mind anyway, so what do you have to lose? My student Will, who had spent his life running from a complicated upbringing in a small Southern town, discovered himself on the porch of his childhood home, swinging in a glider and carving some wood. In the journey, Will was able to give himself over to that comfort with no judgment or fear. In his place of safety, he was inviolate. And in time, because he knew he had that place, he was able to face the demons that had driven him from home and write about them with strength and clarity.

So sit back, relax, and go along for the ride. Notice everything along the way—what colors you see, the length of shadows, the angle of the sun. Notice whether the sounds are near or far, loud or soft, continuous or intermittent. Whether the smells are sharp or subtle. Your senses will lead you more deeply into your experience and keep your anxious conscious mind thoroughly engaged, so your unconscious can surprise you. And isn't that what we're all looking for as writers—the magnificent surprise?

A SAFE PLACE MEDITATION

Now that you're relaxed, not holding on at all, imagine in your mind's eye a safe and beautiful place. It can be a real place, an imaginary place, a place from the past or the present. Don't think about it too much. Whatever comes into your mind, trust it. This is your own safe place, a place of perfect comfort where no harm can come to you. What's around you? Are there plants and trees, familiar furniture, toys? Books? What time of year is it? What time of day? Is the sun shining? Is there a moon and stars? Just notice. How old are you? Are you sitting or standing? How does it feel to be in this safe place? What does the air feel like on your skin? Is it warm, is it cool? Maybe there's a breeze. Are there any sounds? Maybe there's the sound of water, or music, or laughter, or birds. Are there other people around you, or are you alone? Are there smells? Perhaps you smell flowers, or some-

26

thing cooking. Maybe an old familiar fragrance that brings back a happy memory. Just notice. Is there something in this place that you might like to taste? If it's safe to taste it, go ahead. How does it feel on your tongue? Going down your throat? Notice everything. This is your safe place. Explore it with all of your being. Make yourself very comfortable here. Know everything there is to know about this place because it is a place you can come back to time and time again, whenever you feel the need to feel safe. When you're ready, you can begin to write.

How'd it go? Were you able to relax, or did you have a hard time? If you actually found yourself traveling along a path, congratulations! But if you were struggling with resistance or doubt, or you drifted off with little or no memory of where you went, congratulations as well. It doesn't really matter, as long as you wrote from wherever you were in the moment. My student Mark wrote in his first journey: "As the meditation started, I simply drifted into nothing. No field, no forest, no beach. No urban jungle or tranquil garden. Just my own thoughts." For Mark, his own inner voice was a true destination. How many of us complain that we haven't got time to hear ourselves think? "Just my own thoughts" can be a great place to start from.

If you did find yourself in a safe place, I hope

you were able to stay there long enough to get to know it well. Was it a place you recognized, or somewhere completely new? It might have surprised you. Take a moment to notice what this journey can teach you about what you need to feel safe in the here and now— and maybe about what you don't allow in that might make you feel safe. Many of my colleagues and students describe the writing process as some kind of cross between sky-diving without a parachute and leaping off a cliff into shark-infested waters. Being able to create a sense of safety around your own creative process can keep you in your seat long enough to learn how to fly.

Safety has a strong physical component—we experience it in our bodies, our autonomic nervous systems. Notice where in your body you experience safety (breath, belly, heart), and what external elements (time of day, season, quality of light) inform it. These are wonderful things to know for yourself, but these observations will hold true for your characters as well. Learning to examine your responses will sharpen your writing immeasurably.

You may have noticed some changes in your awareness as you allowed yourself to feel safe. Because of the world we live in, most of us are wandering around in a state of high alert—a little adrenaline all of the time. That "code red" keeps our awareness focused on those cues essential for survival at the expense of everything else around us. But when we relax into a feeling of safety, we see things differently. Colors become a little more distinct. We notice the pattern of the wallpaper, feel the texture of the bedspread. It's these details that make for good writing—and, in my opinion, good living.

So what does this "journey" have to do with writing? First of all, finding a safe place inside yourself is one way of finding the courage to deal with the stories that aren't so safe, the stories that are harder (and often more dramatic) to tell. Each of us has countless buried sleights and humiliations that, if brought out of hiding, could illuminate a character or drive a plot forward far more authentically than anything we might imagine.

But we're not just looking for the difficult stories. The journey of searching for a safe place and finally finding one can be a story in itself. Isn't that the thrust of E.M. Forster's *Howards End* or Michael Cunningham's *A Home at the End of the World*? The themes in literature are the themes in life. It's your life. You've lived it. When you're comfortable with experiencing it, it becomes your material for art.

JOURNEY 2

a childhood home

Home is where one starts from.

—T.S. Eliot

For most of my childhood, I lived in a New York apartment overlooking Central Park. From my bedroom window I could see the playground, and the whole room shook whenever the C train rumbled underground. The apartment had nine rooms connected by a series of long hallways. When I was small, its size both tickled and terrified me. If I was alone in my room at one end of the house, I imagined monsters lying in wait at the other end of the hall. But if I had friends from school over, the hallways became a source of delight, a playing field of endless possibilities.

As I grew older, those hallways held different meanings—a dark territory to be navigated softly if I was sneaking in or out, the site where a boy at my first high school party threw up on the carpet and I couldn't get it clean, the runway where I practiced walking in my first pair of high heels.

My dad was a musician, and once a month my parents hosted an evening of chamber music. The apartment would be filled with glorious music, glorious food, and elegant people. But late at night, when everyone had gone home, I could often hear my parents fighting in the bedroom next to mine, and sometimes my father's angry footsteps as he traveled down the hallway and out the front door.

A childhood home is rich with memory—some-

times good, sometimes fearful, but always filled with detail. It's a great place to start, because you know you will find something juicy and emotionally connected. Whether your childhood was the idyllic paradise many of us yearn for, a nightmare of abuse and neglect, or something in between, the material stored in your memory can be mined for your creative work. As my student Andrea says, no one gets out of childhood unscarred, but if you're here to write about it, you clearly lived to tell the tale.

A CHILDHOOD HOME MEDITATION

From this place of relaxation, I want you to begin to take a walk. Just head off in a direction. Putting one foot in front of the other. As you walk, notice what's underneath your feet. Are you walking on sand? On leaves? On earth? On concrete? Just notice and keep on walking. Notice what you're wearing on your feet. Maybe you're barefoot. Maybe you're wearing sneakers or sandals. Maybe you're wearing boots. Just notice and keep on walking. Notice what time of day it is. The temperature. How does the air feel on your skin? Is it warm? Is it cool? Is there a breeze or some rain? Just notice and keep on walking. Notice what's on either side of you. Do you pass a field? Buildings? A seaside? Mountains? Just notice and keep on walking.

As you walk, begin to notice that you are walking back in time. With each step, you walk back another year or two. Notice how your walk changes. Notice if what you were wearing changes. Notice if the environment around you begins to change. And continue to walk.

In a moment, you're going to come to a clearing. And in this clearing you're going to find a childhood home. Some place you lived in as a child.

I want you to step into this clearing now and see this childhood home. Where are you? Are you in the country or in the city? Are there people around you or are you alone?

I want you to slowly approach this childhood home and observe it from the outside. Is there a fence in front of it? A stoop? Are there other houses nearby or does it stand by itself? Is it made of wood? Brick? Can you see the windows?

Notice how you feel when you see this home. Maybe there's a rush of good feeling, of anticipation, or trepidation.

If there's any discomfort, remember that you can always go back to your safe place. There's no need to push to any place of discomfort.

But if you like, approach the front door. Notice what it's made of. What color is it? Notice the doorknob. Is it round and smooth? Is it made of brass or iron? Is there a bell? Are there any sounds coming from inside? Any smells?

Again, noticing how you're feeling, let yourself open the door and step inside. Where are you? Are you in a hallway? A living room? How old are you? I want you to begin to explore this childhood home. Notice what's on the floor. On the walls. Notice if there are other people in the rooms.

Using all your senses, begin to walk through this home, noticing everything. And when you're ready, you can begin to write.

What did your childhood home bring to you? Did you find yourself in a place of sweet memory or at the door to something you'd rather forget? Maybe you were drawn to a scene or a place that is part of your conscious history (somewhere you might have expected to go), or to somewhere that came as a complete surprise. Were you able to inhabit this place with your adult consciousness or were you pulled into the past? What details brought the experience most alive? A smell, an object, a person, the angle of light? Did the attention to detail help to heighten your experience? One of my students began the journey crawling along floorboards in a hallway. She just followed the grain of the wood, the feel of the smooth and rough places, the wisps of dust. Soon she found she had crossed the threshold into her grandmother's room, and from the vantage of her place on the floor, she witnessed a scene that clarified an old and tangled memory.

Traveling to a place filled with so much history can be overwhelming, so don't be surprised if some strong emotions surface. Go easy on yourself. Strong emotion means you've touched something powerful for your own creative process—something you may be able to use now or save for later. Maybe your journey took you to a place of joy or amusement or tenderness. Good experiences are as valuable as difficult ones.

David had lived in many homes as a child, after his father abandoned the family when he was five. He hadn't seen his father since then and had tried to erase him from his memory. The home he landed in was the last place he'd shared with his father. They were at a workbench in the garage, building a model ship together. David wasn't sure if the incident had ever happened, but the sense of connection he felt at that moment opened the door to a host of good memories that had been buried.

Drawing from your own experience doesn't mean you have to write a memoir. Beginning to uncover all the slippery ways memory plays with our idea of truth (and influences our view of reality) can lead to much greater depth and complexity in all of our writing. Your fictional characters may need to borrow liberally from you in order to ground their stories in truth, and the more your own material is available to you, the more you will feel free to play with it.

In literature you might look to Tennessee Williams' play *The Glass Menagerie,* or to Wallace Stegner's remarkable novel *Angle of Repose,* to see how the mem-

ory of a childhood home can be shaped by a master.

When I was studying writing, we were always admonished to "write what you know." But that always felt like a limitation—if we only wrote what we knew, where would the mystery and surprise come from? I think a better thought is: know what you write. If you know it deeply in every cell of your being, because you have rooted it in your own experience, then you can take your reader anywhere and they will believe you.

Most of us read to learn how other people see the world. It's how we discover our common humanity, helping us to feel less isolated in our lives. We all come from somewhere. When you, as a writer, are able to view your history from a fresh perspective, you open the door for each of us to find our own way home.

JOURNEY 3

a messenger

Man is a messenger who forgot the message.

—Abraham Joshua Heschel

've often wondered why life doesn't come with a little how-to manual, a set of driving instructions to get us safely to wherever we want to be going. When I'm stuck with a question I can't seem to answer, it would be great to call up some cosmic customer-service line and ask for technical assistance, though who knows how long I'd be on hold. But looking back over the thorny moments in my past, I have to admit that every time I've truly needed a sign, it has come in one form or another. "A little bird told me." "I heard it through the grapevine." "There was a little voice in my head." "The book just fell off the shelf." When we are in need of guidance, if we are open to what comes our way, a messenger appears. But the truth is, the message we receive is usually a message from our own unconscious, reflected back from the outside world. So what would be available to us if we were able to contact a messenger at will?

In this journey you will be asked to do just that. Maybe you will meet someone from your past, a mentor or a special friend. The message might come from an animal or a bird, as it often does in Native American traditions. Perhaps the message will come more symbolically, something only you would recognize, like a certain piece of clothing or a fragrance. When I was struggling with a piece of writing I was working on, wondering whether it was all right to expose a difficult part of my background, I walked out into my garden for a break. There in front of me was a perfect yellow rose. Yellow roses were my mother's favorite flower. The rose bush had been in my garden for a while, but in this moment, that one perfect rose was a message that spoke to my heart— write what you have to, my mother was saying. I give you permission.

As writers, we must always be on the lookout for messages from our characters, clues to who they are and where they are going. A colleague who found herself stuck at an important juncture in her novel asked her main character to appear in the meditation and lead her to a solution. He did, taking her to a place from his past that she'd never imagined. The scene she witnessed there enabled her to locate the emotions she needed to navigate the next part of her story.

Sometimes receiving the messenger requires subtle perception, sometimes the messenger comes right at you. However your messenger appears, know that it is there to guide you to where you need to be going.

A MESSENGER MEDITATION

From your place of relaxation, begin to head off on a walk. It may be a walk you've taken before, or maybe it's somewhere new. As you walk, notice what you're walking on. Notice what you're wearing on your feet. What time of day is it? Notice the

temperature. How does the air feel on your skin? Are you warm or cold? Are you dressed properly for the temperature?

As you walk, notice what's on either side of you. Is this place new, or have you walked here before? As you pass things, reach out and touch them. Maybe you touch a leaf. A tree. A building. The ocean. Notice how it feels against your fingers. What can you smell? Are there flowers? The smell of something cooking? Burning leaves? Just notice and keep on walking.

As you walk, listen for sounds. Can you hear children's voices? Sirens in the distance? The sound of a crashing sea? Listen to the sounds that are close by. But also listen for the sounds in the distance. In a moment, you will come to a clearing. And as you step into the clearing, across the way, you will see someone coming toward you. As you walk closer, begin to notice who this person is. Is it someone you know? Someone from your past or your present? Maybe it's someone from a movie or a dream. Someone from your imagination. It may even be someone from your future.

Notice what this person is wearing. What color is their hair, their eyes? Are they pleased to see you? How do you feel when you see them? When you meet, what does this person have to say to you?

Find someplace safe and sit down together. Hear what the message is. If you have
something to say to this person, do it now. Perhaps they want to take you somewhere. If you'd
like to and it feels safe, by all means, follow. Notice everything. Use all your senses.

And when you're ready, you can begin to
write.

What form did your messenger take? Was it
someone (or something) you expected, or a complete
surprise?

Mary Anne's messenger came in the form of a
rooster, sitting in the scrubby backyard of a rundown
house. She'd been working on a story that might have
been situated in just such a place, so she followed the
rooster to his perch on a fence. From there she could
observe her protagonist as she went about her morning.
Mary Anne knew the outlines of her story, but from the
rooster's point of view, everything came alive in a new
and magical way. She decided to recast the story with the
rooster at its center, and the whole piece took off.

Sometimes the messenger is clear, but the message a little hard to discern. Joseph recognized his high
school basketball coach immediately, but when he tried
to follow him, he disappeared into a crowded market
place. Joseph darted around the stalls, catching glimpses
only to lose sight again. After a while he gave up the
chase and began to notice the fabulous foods and wares

46

displayed around him. A passionate "foodie," he was dazzled by the variety of exotic produce and spices, and enthralled by the colors and smells that enveloped him. When it came time to write from his journey, he could hardly contain himself. "I guess the message," he said afterward, "was to stop chasing some elusive goal and just notice all the good stuff that's in front of me now."

As writers, we are beholden to the messengers who show up when we sit down to work; it's the willingness to follow the impulse, to not shut out the impression, that leads us into the interior landscape where our stories and characters reside. Harold Pinter, speaking of the genesis of his plays in his Nobel Lecture in 2005, said, "There are no hard distinctions between what is real and what is unreal . . . . Most of the plays are engendered by a line, a word, or an image. The given word is often shortly followed by the image." The line, the word, the image are all messengers from the unconscious that, when followed, lead to the unfolding of a narrative.

JOURNEY 4

an obstacle on the path

Life is full of obstacle illusions.

—Grant Frazier

When I was in my twenties, I had a recurring dream. I'd be walking down a path and in the distance I could hear the sounds of music and laughter. As I continued to walk, the sounds would grow more distinct and soon, ahead of me, I would see a party in full swing. Beautifully dressed people danced to the live music; there were tables of exotic food, a sense of joy and abandon and ease. My heart would race as I approached, drawn in by the sense of celebration. But no matter how many times I approached the scene, there was always a wall of glass between me and the events I was witnessing. I could never join the party.

For years I lived my life with that sense of futility. There was a party going on, but not for me. It obscured my sense of well-being. Even when good things came my way, I was aware of that glass wall. It wasn't until years later that I suddenly woke up to the possibility that I might have a choice. The wall existed in my mind—so what would it take to remove it?

I began to play with the idea. Would I pick up a stone and shatter it? Find a torch and melt it? Maybe I would learn to walk through glass, or maybe, just maybe, I could walk to the edge of the glass and enter from the side.

The point is, life is an obstacle course. Some obstacles are set by the outside world, some we set ourselves, but we are not powerless against these obstacles. The resourcefulness of the creative spirit is a wondrous thing to behold—witness a small child try to open a neatly wrapped package—and our creativity is available to us NO MATTER WHAT.

In this exercise, I invite you to get curious about what the obstacles on your path might look like—what they are made of, how they can be worked with or dismantled, how they serve you, and what they are keeping you from. It's a great exercise for your life and also for your writing—obstacles create conflict, and conflict is the basis of dramatic tension.

AN OBSTACLE ON THE PATH MEDITATION

Set off easily in a direction—any direction. Maybe it's somewhere you've traveled before, maybe it's somewhere new. Again notice what's underneath your feet. Notice whether you're wearing shoes or sandals. Maybe you're barefoot. Be aware of the air as it hits your skin. Is it cool? Is it damp? Maybe it's hot. What time of day is it? Is it dawn or dusk? Deep night or midday? Just notice and keep on walking. Be sure to notice what's on either side of you as you walk. Are there buildings? Fields? Maybe you pass boats or cottages. Perhaps you're in the mountains. Just notice and keep on walking.

Notice if there are any creatures on your path as you walk. Birds or squirrels. Toads or snakes. If you pass a creature, invite it to join you as an ally on your journey. Be aware of the sounds. Are they distant or near? Be aware of the smells. Is there a moss smell? The odor of sulfur? Newly mown grass? A sea breeze? Just notice and keep on walking. In a moment you will come to an obstacle, something that prevents you from continuing on the path. Perhaps it's a wooden fence. Maybe it's made of barbed wire. It might be a brick wall or an enormous fallen tree. Notice the details of its construction.

If it's safe to touch, touch it. If it's wood, is the wood smooth or rough and splintered? If it's made of brick, are the bricks solid or do they crumble? Perhaps it's made of stone. How high is this obstruction? Is there a doorway? Can you see what's on the other side? How are you going to get from this side of the fence or wall to the other side? Perhaps you'll climb the wall, or maybe you'll scramble under. Maybe the gate will open or maybe you'll have to find the key. Whatever you have to do to get to the other side, I'd like you to do it now. Notice what the effort feels like. It may be hard, it may be easy, but you will get to the other side. When you've reached the other side, notice where you are. Begin to explore this environment. Are you inside or out? Are you alone or with others? Can you see a long distance ahead or is this just the next step? What does this place mean to you?

If you can, look back behind you and see where you've come from to get to this place. When you're ready, you can begin to write.

OK. So did you have to climb Mt. Everest? Some of our obstacles appear that large, others are little tacks on the road that blow out our tires. Whatever form your obstacle takes, it still holds the potential to keep you from your dreams. It also holds the potential to force you to decide how much you want something. Are your obstacles sometimes opportunities? Anthony, an adventure writer whose eyesight had been impaired in an accident, encountered a mountain of darkness in his journey. At first it seemed impassable, but reminding himself that it was "just in his head," he donned his skis and slalomed to the other side. After the initial fear, he found that his instincts kicked in and he was able to navigate the terrain. As he traveled, his eyes grew accustomed to the dark so he could see more clearly. He came back from the journey determined to write about the challenges of "adventuring" with physical limitations.

Getting to the other side of anything can be exhausting, but it's usually the kind of exhaustion that comes with the relief of accomplishment. Often the hardest part of getting to the other side is getting out of your own way. If you found that it took a lot of effort to get past your obstacle, reward yourself. It's a big deal. Chances are that obstacle's been around in one form or another for a long time. You might want to make note of what you think it's been keeping you from, and watch over the next several weeks to see if things have shifted.

Maybe it was easy to get to the other side. We often create "false obstacles" to avoid moving forward or making a change, and much like the monsters that lurk in our bedrooms when we're small, they disappear when we turn on the light.

The overcoming of obstacles is a crucial element in writing. Without obstacles Romeo and Juliet would be married and living in the suburbs of Verona, and Scarlett O'Hara would be hosting teas. The struggle to overcome and grow is the most basic human story. So honor your obstacles for keeping you human and know that you've just given yourself an open road to the next adventure.

JOURNEY 5

a fork in the road

When you come to a fork in the road, take it.

—Yogi Berra

Several years ago one of my students, Lisa, called in a panic. She'd been offered two splendid career opportunities and couldn't decide which one to take. They paid the same, and each offered the kind of challenging work she'd been longing for. An embarrassment of riches. So why the panic? Because, she wailed, if she chose one, she'd be shutting the door on the other. What if she chose the wrong one and her destiny was altered forever? She was in such a state of paralysis that she was considering turning down both jobs and staying where she was. It seemed easier not to make a move than to have to choose.

Inspired by Lisa's quandary, I led one of my classes on a journey to a fork in the road. They were asked to choose a direction and travel down it, exploring the path and their feelings about having to choose. Then I asked them to come back and take the other fork. What a revelation. It had never occurred to any of them that once they had made a choice, the other path might still be open to them. By traveling both paths, they were able to gain more information about the risks and rewards of each choice. Lisa found enough clues about her own situation to accept one of the offers, knowing that if it didn't work out, she could always take another road.

Life is a series of choices. Each one brings us something that furthers our growth, but if it's a kind of growth that we're not happy with, we're not without options. In this exercise I invite you to travel to your own fork in the road. It may be a situation from your present life, a choice you made in the past (and might like to do over), or something surprising. Just know that each of these paths will take you to the same destination—your future. Whichever one you travel, the choice is yours.

A FORK IN THE ROAD MEDITATION

From your place of relaxation, begin to take a walk, reminding yourself to be aware of what you're walking on, what you're wearing, what the atmosphere is. Notice if it's different from other walks you've taken. Perhaps you're cold, perhaps it's raining. Maybe you're hot and you need to take your jacket off. Maybe there's a cool breeze. Just notice and keep on walking. Notice what's on either side of you. Is this a new place, or some place you've traveled before? If you've been here before, notice what's different. Are you in a different season? Are the houses painted a different color? Are there different animals? Different flowers? Different people? Just notice and keep on walking. Notice what you smell, and notice what you hear. If there is something you'd like to taste, taste it. In a moment, you will come to a fork in the road. To the

right is a path that leads up, to the left a path that leads down. Stand for a moment at this crossroads. For now, which path do you want to choose? You can always go back later and choose the other path. When you've made your decision, step onto the new path. What are you walking on? Has the terrain changed? Perhaps you were walking on earth, and now you are walking on sand. Maybe you're on a staircase. What's it made out of? Is the path curved or straight? What's on either side of you? If you were in the country before, are you in the city now? Just notice and keep on walking. Notice how the quality of light changes. Are you moving from light to dark, or dark to light? Full sun to shadow? Just notice and keep on walking. Soon you will come to the end of this path. Where are you? Are you inside or out? What can you see from where you stand? Are you alone, or are there others there with you? Maybe there are animals. Explore this environment using all your senses. Why have you chosen to come here? If there are other people here, what do they have to say to you or you to them? When you're ready, you can begin to write.

Was making a choice as hard for you as it was for Lisa? Did knowing that this was just an exercise (and knowing that you could come back and do it again) give you permission to just choose and let go? What's most important is noticing what the experience was for you. If you found yourself dreading the idea of making a choice, that dread holds a wealth of information—about you, certainly, but also about what a character might feel. If the dread makes your breathing shallow or makes you want to run, these are wonderful ways of expressing that emotion. Maybe having a choice filled you with exhilaration or a sense of adventure. Noticing our own reactions provides an endless source of information about the human experience. You're your own best experiment. Research well.

Now here's the fun part. What would happen if you went back and chose the other path? Even the thought of that possibility can change your perspective. Maybe there are choices you've made in your life that you'd like to revisit—the proverbial "road not taken." This exercise is a way to explore not only what you know about your life's choices, but what you might be afraid to know. Unexplored places in our histories are unexplored places in our psyches—whole continents of material available for our life and our work. Make a list of choices you've made and do this exercise over and over—you'll be amazed at how much territory you can reclaim.

The notion of a fork in the road is the structural basis of much great literature—the fateful choice that sets in motion a series of inevitable consequences shaping the characters' destinies. What would have become of Heathcliff in *Wuthering Heights* had Cathy not married Edgar Linton? Or Frodo in *The Lord of the Rings* if he'd refused the mission to destroy the ring? In writing, the fateful choice is usually the most dramatic and compelling. But it's not the only story.

Our belief that our choices seal our fate can shut down the creative process before it ever begins. What do we writers do but make choices? Who will be the narrator? What scenes to include? Which story (of the endless ones in our head) do we commit to? One friend, under contract for her second novel, realized after six months of writing that she was going to have to go back and tell her story from another perspective. But even in the midst of her disappointment, she knew that everything she'd learned going down the "wrong" road would add depth and texture to the finished piece.

Writing is not for the faint of heart, but then neither is life. It takes courage to set out not knowing what lies ahead. But knowing you can make another choice is like having GPS—no matter how lost you might be, you can find another path to wherever it is you want to go.

JOURNEY 6

a distant sound

All the sounds of the earth are like music.

—Oscar Hammerstein II

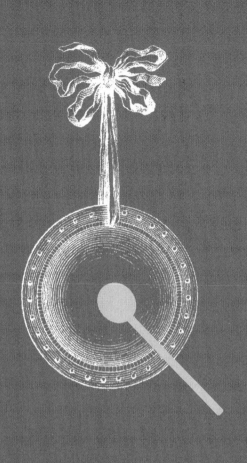

Gong. Gong. Gong. I find myself sitting in the foothills of the Himalayas. Ahead of me, in the distance, the sun rises over Mt. Kanchenjunga. Below me is a monastery. I can see the monks in their maroon-and-saffron robes as they navigate the elegant dance of monastic debate in the courtyard between the buildings. Colorful prayer flags dot the landscape, flap-flapping in the breeze. The gong rings again and I rise, moving toward its call. I notice that I, too, am wearing saffron robes. I look at my feet—sturdy oxblood shoes. I look at my hands. They are large and flat, a leathery dark brown. As I begin to move, it becomes clear that I am an old monk, and the gong that I hear is the gong that has called me to prayer for most of my life.

It has been said that one of the great paths to enlightenment is the path of sound. I can't verify that statement, but I do know that a powerful sound can draw you instantly to another time and place. I have only to hear the tinny music of a carousel to land me back in my childhood in Paris, or the rattle of the subway to bring me to my grandparents on Jerome Avenue in the Bronx.

One afternoon while I was teaching a workshop in my home, the neighbor's dogs began to howl. My students were deep in the meditation and I was concerned that the din would break their concentration, so I suggested they acknowledge the sound and incorporate it into their inner experience. The results were astonishing. One student was pulled back to a memory of a wounded dog he and his brothers had found in a field and rescued, another recalled being attacked by a dog. For still another, the barking became background noise, and she found herself drawn to a first kiss that happened in an alley behind a kennel.

Sometimes the "sound" is an absence of sound. Writer Annie Dillard, in *Teaching a Stone to Talk*, experiences a familiar landscape in a whole new way due to a lack of sound: "The silence gathered and struck me. It bashed me broadside from the heavens above me like yard goods; ten acres of fallen, invisible sky choked the fields. The pastures on either side of the road turned green in a surrealistic fashion, monstrous, impeccable, as if they were holding their breaths."

Following a sound focuses your concentration so you are less likely to notice if the world around you is shifting. In life this may be dangerous, but for your work and your exploration it's invaluable. Slipping out of the grasp of ordinary reality and into the realm of the imagination is, for most of us, a tricky business. Sound can carry you past your resistances.

In this journey I invite you to stay open to all the sounds you encounter, letting them drift through your consciousness until that one particular sound calls to you. It may be the sound of a cricket or the honk of a horn—it doesn't matter. Whatever it is, it's a call to enter your creative well.

A DISTANT SOUND MEDITATION

Now that you're relaxed, begin to take your walk, noticing what's under neath your feet. Notice the sound it makes as you walk. Is there the crunch of gravel or the rustle of leaves? The squish of soggy earth? How do you walk? Heel first and then your toe? Your whole foot? What are you wearing on your feet? If you're barefoot, what can you feel? Sharp pebbles, soft petals, warm sand, ooze? Just notice and keep on walking.

Are you walking in the light of day? Under a starry sky? How does the air feel on your skin? Is it cool? Are you sweating? Maybe a breeze blows through your hair. Just notice and keep on walking.

Notice what's on either side of you as you walk. Are objects close to you or far away? Do you feel crowded, or is there a sense of space? Are you walking somewhere you've been before, or is this a new place? Just notice and keep on walking.

Notice the smells. If you smell flowers, what kind of flowers? The soft scent of roses? The saturated sweetness of honeysuckle? Maybe it's lilac blossoms, or a eucalyptus tree. Are these summer smells or winter smells? Maybe it's the smell of smoke from chimneys, or the smell of a pine forest. Whatever the smell, notice how it makes you feel.

Does it remind you of another time and place? Just notice and keep on walking.

In a moment, you will hear a sound way off in the distance. Begin to follow that sound. It may take you off the path and onto new terrain. Wherever that sound is coming from, I want you to begin to follow now and see where it leads you. Just travel the distance until the sound grows closer, louder, more distinct. What can you hear? Why is the sound calling to you? Where is it leading you?

In a moment, you will find the source of the sound. Notice where you are. Are you inside or outside? Alone or with others? Why has this particular sound called you to this place and to this time?

Explore, using all of your senses. And when you're ready, you can begin to write.

Was the sound that called you gentle and insistent or loud and sharp? Maybe it lulled you into a fond memory or dropped you suddenly into an alien landscape. As you read what you wrote, notice if there is a difference in the quality of your writing as the experience shifts. Your language may seem sharper, more precise, the images a little clearer. Sometimes the heightened concentration of one sense increases the awareness of all the senses: colors are brighter, smells more intense, your

skin more alive.

Louise, an emergency room nurse, heard the sound of an ambulance. Oh no, she thought, I can't escape my daily life! But she stayed with the sound anyway. It brought her to the inside of an ambulance when she was a small child. She was the patient, struggling to stay conscious after a severe allergy attack. The sound of a woman's voice kept insisting that she was going to be all right, that she had nothing to fear. Louise knew if she followed the voice, she would stay alive. She felt a wave of profound gratitude for this being, and gradually, by the end of the meditation, had been able to see the woman's face and feel the touch of her hand, willing Louise to stay alive. Later, she checked with her mother—indeed, she had had a severe allergic reaction when she was barely three, and a female emergency technician had arrived with the ambulance. Louise gained a sense of where her own life's calling had come from, and of the power of words to heal.

A sound can lead you to an experience from which to write, or become the experience itself, as in the Pablo Neruda poem that begins:

Your laugh: it reminds me of a tree
fissured by a lightning streak, by a silver bolt
that drops from the sky, splitting the poll,
slicing the tree with its sword.

Recently I traveled to India, visiting many Hindu and Jain temples. In each temple was a loud bell that worshippers rang as they entered to pray. An old priest in Delhi explained that the sound of the bell cleared

the mind of ordinary reality to prepare it for spiritual insight. Each of our senses is a doorway to rich experience, but I'll go with that old priest's advice. There's nothing like sound to clear the mind of ordinary reality, and prepare it for creative expression.

JOURNEY 7

a bridge

He that would be a leader must be a bridge.

—Welsh proverb

H ere I am. Stuck in my life. The dishes need washing. The bills need to be paid. The dog needs a walk. And I need to be writing.

Here I am. Stuck in the city, longing to be sitting on a beach in the tropics, sipping coconut milk.

Here I am, stuck in a job I hate, afraid to imagine there might be something else out there for me.

Here I am. Stuck wherever I am, and there's somewhere else I long to be. Buddhist practice might suggest I stay right where I am and see what comes up— and there's a lot to be said for that. But my creative spirit tells me I need an adventure.

Somewhere just beyond your grasp is something you've been longing for: a new job, a new relationship, a new way of seeing yourself in the world. It exists as a kind of distant island, isolated and somewhat unreachable. Maybe you don't have a clear vision of what it is, just a sense that it exists. The question, of course, is how do you get there from here?

In ordinary reality building a bridge is a huge undertaking. Even a simple rope bridge needs sophisticated understanding of the principles of weight and tension. But metaphorically, bridges can be built in a moment.

Peter, a television producer, had been struggling with his deep dissatisfaction at work. He had chosen a career in the entertainment industry because he thought it would fulfill him, but he found himself mired in the business aspects, unable to "bridge" the creative gap. No matter how he viewed it, he couldn't see a way to make a change.

As a child he had spent his summers on the island of Martinique with his maternal grandmother. On his journey, he found himself standing on the back lot of the studio where he worked. In front of him was a small wooden bridge, a bridge he recognized from the island. He took his shoes off and stepped onto the bridge, crossing easily back to his childhood in his grandmother's house. Lured by the smell of her wonderful cooking, he sat down at the table and listened to his grandmother's fabulous stories of the islands. Something in one of those stories hit a nerve, and before long Peter developed it into a film script, opening the door to his moving out of producing and into television writing. He never actually left his studio lot, but his entire world there changed.

A bridge offers a practical way to close the gap between limitation and possibility by creating a pathway for change, movement, new choices, and perspectives. It offers a way out and, most importantly, it offers a way to return and put those new perspectives into practice.

In this meditation I invite you to start where you are. No matter how uncomfortable, dull, flat, or chaotic, the place you are starting from is simply the place where the bridge originates. Once you have crossed to the other side, it may look and feel quite different.

A BRIDGE MEDITATION

Now that you're relaxed, you can begin to take
your walk. If you like, you can travel the path
you've traveled before, noticing what's different
this time. Does this path change with the seasons,
with the time of day, with your frame of mind? Or
maybe you're on a new path. If so, be sure to give
yourself time to explore. Notice what you're walking on, what sounds you make, what you pass on
either side of you. Be aware of the temperature,
of the feel of the air on your skin. Are you warm or
cold? Is the path lit by moonlight? By a bright blaz-
ing sun? Are there places where you're shaded?
And others where you're exposed? What sounds
can you hear? Birds? Cars? Music? Voices? A
babbling brook? What smells? Pine needles? In-
cense? Gardenia? The smell of bacon cooking? A
campfire? Just notice and keep on walking. Notice what insects you see as you travel. Are there
water bugs and beetles? Ladybugs, black flies,
mosquitoes, lacewings? Just notice and keep on
walking. Notice if there are animals, and notice
if they are fearful or if they approach you. In a
moment you will come to the end of your path.
Across the way the path continues, but you need
to get from here to there. Search along this pe-

rimeter and see if you can find a bridge. It may be made of stone or wood. Maybe it's old. Maybe it's new and beautifully engineered. Maybe you have to build a bridge. If so, what do you build it with? How will you make sure it's secure? How will you get from here to the other side? When you have found or built your bridge, begin to cross it. At the halfway point, look back and see where you are coming from, then turn and continue on your way to the other side. Where are you? Where have you arrived? Are you somewhere you've been before, or is this place entirely new? Notice what you're wearing. How old are you? In this new place, are there other people? Do they recognize you, or are you a stranger? Explore your new environment. Make yourself at home. See if there are people here who want to take you in. Where do you belong here? Why have you come to this place? When you have found the answers, you can begin to write.

What form did your bridge take? Was it a huge steel suspension bridge, or a simple construction of wood and rope? Perhaps it spanned an ocean, or maybe just lifted you over a stream. For Janice, it came as a rainbow. She was sitting on the porch of her son's house, holding her new granddaughter in her lap. Suddenly a rainbow appeared. At first she wasn't sure what to do. It didn't seem like a real bridge, more like a flight of fancy. And what to do about the baby? Finally, she reasoned, it was just a journey in her mind. So, baby in her arms, she stepped to the edge of the rainbow. It was surprisingly solid. As she began to climb, she realized that it was moving. She didn't have to make any effort at all, the bridge was transporting her. And she understood in that moment that she could stop worrying about what the future would bring. She could trust that she would be carried through the next stage of her life, that this wonderful child would be a part of that process, and that something that at first might not seem solid could turn out to be just what she was looking for. She never landed anywhere on her journey. The rainbow—her bridge—was destination enough.

In writing, bridges are often about transitions, a way of taking disparate characters or episodes and bringing them together in the service of your story. Sometimes the bridge can show you how two stories relate by literally moving you from one to the other. Sometimes the quality of the bridge—whether it swings gently or is solid and reinforced—can give you a sense of how to navigate and pace the progression from one event to another.

Getting through life (and through the creative process) is about a series of "gettings" from here to there. No destination is unreachable, if we are willing to take the first step. There's a reason "building bridges" is so often used as a metaphor—in relationships, in the peacemaking process, in community development: it works.

Toward the end of Mark Helprin's *Winter's Tale,* a builder of bridges has cause to reflect on the meaning of his work: "It had taken him ages to realize that he had to make a bridge of light without a discernible end. Before that, he had built wonders of lovely proportion and airy grace . . . which were in themselves an ideal synthesis of rising and falling, aspiration and despair, rebellion and submission, pride and humility." The bridging of worlds is such a central image to the book that Helprin begins his manuscript with a separate page that reads: "I have been to another world, and come back. Listen to me."

As writers, it is often our responsibility to notice where we (and the world around us) have reached the limit of our available resources, and to build the bridge so that we can cross over into the next domain and bring its riches back.

JOURNEY 8

a body of water

It furthers one to cross the great water.

—I CHING #13

Years ago, against all odds, I became certified as a scuba diver. At the time, I was a land-locked shallow breather prone to panic attacks that left me choking on air. But I found myself shooting a commercial at a Caribbean resort with a group of intrepid models who were going to try diving. After conquering my fear of wearing a bathing suit in the company of models, I strapped on a tank and followed the divemaster off the shore and into the deep. I was captivated. We traveled slowly, starting from water we could stand in and gradually moving out until we reached a depth of about thirty feet. Our leader had equipped us with plastic bags filled with bread, and as we swam we fed the brilliantly colored fish who followed us. The fish were so beautiful, the coral reefs so alive and exotic, that I forgot to be afraid. I had entered a world I never knew existed and I was determined to come back.

I am not a natural athlete or a great swimmer, so dive certification was hard for me. But the vision of what I had experienced kept me going. I've since logged some ninety dives, swimming with turtles and dolphins, watching moray eels and octopuses float free at night. Diving has slowed me down, deepened my breath, and helped me to move past my own perceived limitations. I have dived with teenagers, old people, and even paraplegics. And yes, on occasion, I have dived with sharks.

Here's what a body of water offers that you can't find on land:

1. You can jump in.
2. You can just float and be carried along.
3. You can swim upstream, against the current.
4. You can mingle with sea creatures.
5. You can face your fear of the deep.
6. You can go back to a womb-like state.
7. You are out of your element.

Rivers, oceans, streams, ponds, swimming pools, and even puddles are amazing places to meet your unconscious in its purest form. Water breeds life, and life breeds creativity. Even a stagnant pool is full of potential! In this journey I invite you to do more than just skim the surface—and if you find that you're not quite ready to dive in, at least try to get your feet wet.

A BODY OF WATER MEDITATION

From your place of deep relaxation, begin to take a slow and easy walk, noticing what's underneath your feet. Are you walking on gravel or sand? Grass? What are you wearing on your feet? Notice the time of day, the temperature, the quality of the air. How does it feel on your skin? Maybe it's warm and moist. Maybe there's snow, or a hot dry breeze. Just notice and keep on walking.

As you walk, notice what you pass on either side. Buildings, fields, mountains, the ocean. Do you pass people? Animals? Birds? Just notice and keep on walking.

Notice the smells in the air. Listen for sounds.

In a moment you will come to a body of water. Perhaps you're near the ocean, a mountain stream, a lake, or a pond. Maybe it's a swamp. As you approach this body of water, notice what's around you. What kind of vegetation can you find?

Are you standing in wet sand? Gooey mud? Maybe you're on a dock or in a boat.

If you're at the ocean, is it clear and calm? A crashing surf? If you're at a lake, is it frozen? Are there fish?

In a moment, I'm going to ask you to set out on this body of water. Perhaps you'll decide to swim. Maybe you'll dive in from a high cliff. Maybe you'll take a boat or a raft. Perhaps you'll find yourself on the back of a turtle. However you choose to navigate these waters, set off now and see which way the journey takes you.

Notice if you're traveling out toward another land mass or if you're staying on the water.

If you want to drop down, give yourself equipment so that you can leave and see what's underneath. Notice what passes on either side of

you as you travel. Notice the quality of the air. If you've started in one place, where are you traveling to? Notice the shifts of light, the different smells. Notice particularly what creatures and visitors come to join you.

And when you're ready, you can begin to write.

What sort of water did you find? Perhaps it was a vast and open sea, or maybe a backyard pool. Was the water clear or murky? Were there tides or rapids, or maybe a gentle rolling wave? It may have been deep or shallow, warm or cold. Were you comfortable entering into the water, or did you find another way to traverse it? Water is a traditional metaphor for the unconscious mind, so be sure to notice anything that might have symbolic value—a boat, a person, a creature, the view.

Allison had a lifetime fear of sharks. When she was a child, she refused to take baths because she was sure that a shark would come up from the drain and eat her. As an adult that fear translated into all kinds of limitations she placed on herself—an unwillingness to confront authority, to take even moderate physical and emotional risks, even to enter the water when her friends went swimming or kayaking. In her journey she traveled back to the bathtub of her childhood (to a Body of Bathwater) but this time as an adult. She dared the sharks to show themselves, and what appeared was a flotilla of rubber sharkies. Once she got over the surprise, she

let herself play with them, seeing her terror for what it was—a childhood fantasy.

In some cultures water is considered to have healing properties. Rosella, a cancer survivor who had just completed chemotherapy, found herself at a waterfall in her native Costa Rica. As she dove into the clear pool beneath the falls, she felt all the fear and the toxins that were stored in her body wash away. For the first time in months, she experienced a sense of well-being.

A body of water can be an invaluable setting for a piece of writing. It's the only other place besides land (and outer space) that actually exists, and yet characters will always be a little out of their natural element. The surface of water can appear one way, while the depths are vastly different. Its mythic resonance is ingrained in our psyches, so the metaphor is implied and never has to be stated. Perhaps this is why so much great literature has been set in and around a body of water. From the endless ocean of Yann Martel's *Life of Pi* to Huck Finn's Mississippi River to the sea that spawned *Moby Dick* or the pond of *The Wind in the Willows*, water has provided an unparalleled medium for the creative imagination. And, as Mark Twain said, "Water, taken in moderation, cannot hurt anybody."

JOURNEY 9

a precipice
(a leap of faith)

All growth is a leap in the dark,

a spontaneous unpremeditated act

without benefit of experience.

—Henry Miller

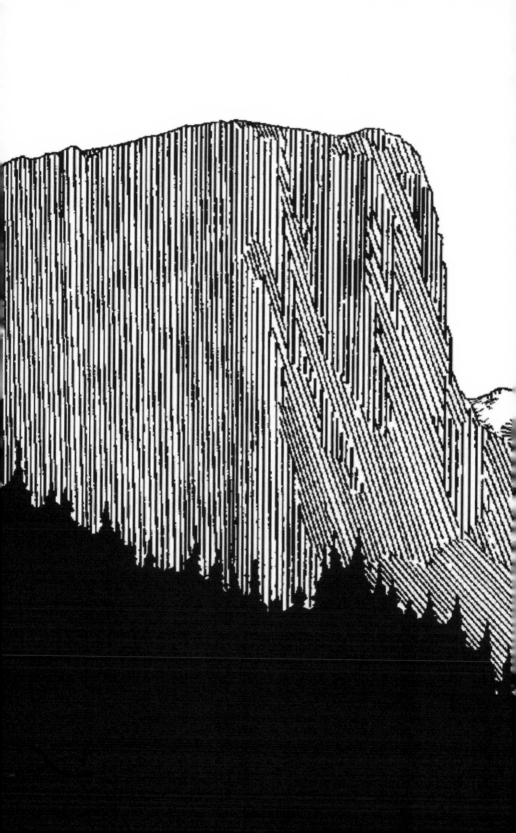

I am curled up tight in a ball under the covers. Outside me, I know, is the home I love, my garden, my friends, the sense of security I have worked so hard to create. A sense of security I am trying hard to hold onto. But here's what I know, here's what is keeping me under the covers because I don't want to know it: I have come to the edge again. It's time for the next leap of faith.

I fight it. I am older now, I say. When I was young, the edge signaled the next adventure, a chance to jump off and try my wings. These days I think: I've done this before. I'm tired. Haven't I grown and risked enough? I'll just sit here in a place of ease and watch this life go by.

That's when I pull off the covers. Because, of course, I can't watch my life go by. I need to live it. Fully. Whether I am 20 or 40 or 75, I will always want to be part of the next big adventure. And that will always require my willingness to walk to whatever edge I've been avoiding and take the next leap of faith. We humans are creatures of habit. We like to live in a known and measured world. We erect our fences, circle our wagons, mark our boundaries, and dig in our heels. This is it, we like to say: this is my life. But some of us, those called to a creative path, know that the edge is always there and that, inevitably, we will have to move toward it if we are to continue to grow.

This leap of faith thing can get tricky, though. Growth requires risk, but risk can sometimes lead us into foolish and even dangerous behavior. So how do we navigate the territory between danger and risk? Practice and observation are great places to start.

In this meditation, try staying open to the feelings associated with coming to the edge. Some of you, like my student Diana, may race easily to the top of a mountain and throw yourself off, sure you will land safely in a big pile of snow. But for others, coming to the edge may bring up feelings of concern or even terror. Stay with it. You may discover that what feels like terror in the moment can become excitement or even ecstatic joy if you let it reveal itself without any judgment. As an actor, every time I step onto a stage, I experience terror. But I have learned from experience that as soon as I embrace it, the terror turns to anticipation, and the nerves become the fuel for my work. Now I'm only really scared when I don't feel the fear—some essential ingredient of the creative process is missing!

A PRECIPICE MEDITATION

Now that you're relaxed, you can set off on your way. Maybe this time you're running. Maybe you're skipping. Maybe you're walking slowly. Maybe today you're on a bicycle. But however you're traveling, notice the road you're traveling on. What is

it made of? Is it concrete or earth? Hard or soft?
Smooth or rough as you travel across it?

Notice what passes you on either side. If
you're moving quickly and things are whizzing by,
what sound do they make as you go by them?

What sensation do you get from the blur?
Are the colors soft or distinct? If you're moving
slowly, notice the details. If you walk by trees,
what shape are the leaves? Are some leaves green
and others colored? What size are they? What's
the bark on the trees like? If you're walking in the
city, what buildings do you pass? Are they old
brick buildings, or sleek new skyscrapers? Are the
streets you walk on clean or filled with litter?

Notice the faces of people as you pass. Do
they seem relaxed and joyful? Tense and frightened? Just notice, and keep on walking.

Notice what you smell. Notice what you
hear. Notice how you're feeling. Are you light of
heart, or heavy? Are you moving forward with joy
and expectation? Anticipation? Or is there some
fear, something holding you back? Just notice
and keep on walking. In a moment you are going
to come to the end of the path. Just like that. It
stops. You are at the edge, the end of this road.
Where are you? On a cliff overlooking the sea?
At the end of a pier? Maybe before you lies darkness, or bright light. Notice what shape your edge

seems to take. Is it sharp and ragged or soft and smooth? Does it seem to slope gently, or is there a precipitous drop? Can you see what lies beyond it? Notice what feelings come up as you draw near to the edge. And notice how the feelings change if you just allow yourself to observe them and breathe. In a moment I'm going to ask you to consider walk ing to the edge and jumping off—taking that leap of faith. If that doesn't feel right, stay where you are. Getting to the edge may be all the experience you need or want right now. Observe yourself as you make the decision—is it easy or hard? Maybe you just lift off, maybe you pull back in hesitation, afraid to let go. But if you've decided you're going to, make that leap now. When you're ready, you can begin to write.

Were you able to make a leap, or did you find yourself holding back? If you didn't leap, try to notice why. Was it simply fear? Great! You can always try again. Or was it something else—some instinct that leaping right now might not be wise? For those of us who leap too easily, NOT taking the leap can be the most daring choice. Holding back can be as valuable as leaping, because it allows you to really notice all the steps leading up to a decision.

Adam's edge brought him to a sheer cliff. An avid extreme-sportsman, he actually laughed when he saw it. This was it? No problem. He donned some climbing gear and prepared to rappel down. But, surprisingly, he found himself too frightened to make the next step. He imagined more and better equipment, reminded himself of his strength and experience, and still he couldn't begin. Confused, he sat down and waited. He noticed the grass he was sitting on, the shadow of the moon over the distant mountains, the soft pile of his jacket. Soon he began to relax. Why make the descent, he thought. It's beautiful right here. He drifted off into a half-sleep. In his dream-state a young woman came to him, and he agreed to let her guide him down. "It was the first time I had let a woman take the lead," he said afterwards. "And it wasn't in the least bit frightening—in fact, I enjoyed it!"

Sometimes the precipice defines two realities, opening a glimpse into other truths. Sometimes it shows us our limitations, the edge we need to explore. In writing, this edge can bring clarity, a sense of purpose, and urgency to your language. There's a kind of "no kidding" quality that can call you forth into the unknown, the uncharted places in your imagination. Taking the leap of faith, when you are sure it is the right step, can lead you to a sense of freedom and power that will send you racing to the page.

The image of the precipice abounds in literature—from the spiritual metaphor of W. Somerset Maugham's *The Razor's Edge* to the leaping through portals into other worlds of Philip Pullman's *His Dark Materials* trilogy. But always, always, it is an opportunity to step beyond the boundaries of the known world and into the mystery beyond.

JOURNEY 10

an inner garden

Mary, Mary, quite contrary, how does your garden grow?

—English nursery rhyme

grew up in New York—concrete-born and -raised. I spent summers at the beach (and can dig my toes into the sand with the best of them), but that was the limit of my connection to nature. That I now tend a garden filled with organic vegetables and exquisite flowers is testament to the power of the creative imagination.

I was in a difficult place in my marriage when I first decided to journey to my own "inner garden." Not surprisingly, I found that the landscape was barren—I was feeling out of touch with my life, and my garden showed it. Instead of beautiful flowers, I saw empty beds with a few wispy weeds. The earth was dry and parched, and although I was seeing in color, there was no color to see. No cute little Disney creatures showed up to cheer me. There was no running water, not even a place to sit down. I was bereft. I had known on some level that things were out of balance, but the extent of it shocked me. I vowed to return to my garden on a daily basis and see if I could make something wonderful grow.

Each day in my meditation I brought something new with me. At first it was tools and bags of dirt so I could amend the soil, then flowers and plants, just seedlings. I installed a watering system, and for good measure created a waterfall and a pond. Animals and birds began to show up, and as the plants began to grow and bloom, I found myself creating places to sit and read, paths to wander down. My garden became a work of art. It was a place I looked forward to visiting at the end of a day in the city, and all I had to do was sit down and close my eyes.

In my "outside" life, I had begun to read books on gardening, drawn to illustrations and photographs that fueled my imaginary project. I began to long for the country, for walks in the woods and the smell of night-blooming jasmine. I moved to a loft with a roof deck and began a garden there, a little oasis that bloomed each spring and summer.

But the power of my project was bigger than that. It took several years to land myself in a cottage on a hillside in Southern California with a small backyard. My first month I cut a little patch out of the lawn and planted six-packs of perennials I'd picked up at the nursery. They looked tiny and fragile, a little like I, a newly transplanted New Yorker, felt, but by spring they had flowered. I planted some more—bare root roses, French lavender, bulbs—and soon I was having to prune them back. The second summer, I stood in the garden with a group of new friends and marveled at a six-foot sunflower that had volunteered. "It's your guardian angel," one friend said, and maybe it was.

These days the garden has quadrupled in size, and when I come home at night, I pick my own supper. No longer the city slicker I was raised to be, I am living the life I have always craved.

Our inner and outer lives reflect each other, and a change in one can open the door for change in the other. In this exercise, I invite you to explore what your inner landscape has to tell you about where you are today—no judgment, no sense of good or bad, just what is. Because, as the renowned Buddhist nun Pema Chödrön teaches, you must start where you are. Then you can return as often as you like and create what your heart desires.

AN INNER GARDEN MEDITATION

Starting from your relaxed place, try to imagine that you're about to enter a garden. It could be a garden from your life or a garden from your imagination. Perhaps it's a garden you've seen in a photograph. Stand on the outside of the garden. Is there an iron gate, or a white wooden fence? A hedge? Can you see into the garden from where you're standing, or is it blocked from your view? Just notice. In a moment you will enter this garden, but before you do, observe yourself. How old are you? What are you wearing? Are you carrying anything in your hand? Just notice. Step into the garden now, and begin to walk down the path. Notice what's underneath your feet. Are there cobblestones? A lawn? Perhaps you're in a flowerbed. As you walk along this path, observe what's on each side. Are there trees? Are there flowers? Hedges? What time of year is it? Is the sun warm on your shoulders? Are there colorful pansies and peonies in bloom, or is everything barren? Just notice and keep walking. What kind of smells are there? Does the earth smell rich and moist? Is there the sweet aroma of fruit trees? As you walk down this path, observe the colors. Reds, blues, greens, purples. Orange. Yellow. White. Perhaps there's no color at all.

As you continue to walk, notice if there's water anywhere in this garden. Perhaps there's a stream, a fountain, a birdbath, a well. Find a place to sit and see if the garden looks different from this new perspective. Are you on a bench? Under a tree? Notice if there are any small creatures around. Birds? Squirrels? Butterflies? Insects? Observe each creature, and see what they gravitate toward. See what they do. Listen to their sounds. Notice if there's a structure in the garden—a shed, a cupola, a teahouse, any place of shelter. As you sit here and observe, make note of what is missing. Is there not enough color? Not enough sound? Not enough light or shelter? Just notice, and as you notice imagine that it is possible to change this garden. You can plant new plants and flowers, bring in a source of water, build a shelter, attract small creatures. It can be an ongoing project, just as the planting of a real garden evolves over time. You can come back as often as you'd like and continue to work in this garden to create it the way

you want it to be. When you're ready, you can begin to write.

So, how did your garden grow? (Sorry!) Maybe it was filled with riotous color, or perhaps you found it dormant. Cathy, who had stopped writing poetry when her children were born, found an empty patch of newly turned soil on her journey. At first she thought to work it herself, but then she got a better idea: she invited her children in, gave them seeds and tools, and sat down on a bench to write while her children planted.

How we find our garden can tell us a lot about what's going on in our emotional lives. In *The Secret Garden,* Frances Hodgson Burnett's classic story, the unhappy young heroine, Mary, first sees the garden in winter. "All the ground was covered with grass of a wintry brown." But Mary is also able to see that "their thin gray or brown branches and sprays looked like a sort of hazy mantle . . . which made it all look so mysterious." Even out of bloom, a garden holds the possibility of beauty. Shades of gray and brown are subtle colorations, but subtlety is a much-coveted skill for both life and writing.

What did the state of your garden reflect about your inner life? Maybe you noticed new growth, signs of spring that surprised and delighted you. Whatever the case, check in with what it's telling you. Metaphor is the language of the unconscious. A garden is a classic metaphor for growth or decay. Lest you think it's a soft and fuzzy one, listen to how Shakespeare describes the sad

state of England in *Richard II*:

> Our sea-walled garden, the whole land, Is
> full of Weeds, her fairest flowers choked
> up, Her fruit trees all Unpruned, her
> hedges ruined, Her knots disordered, And
> her wholesome herbs Swarming with cat-
> erpillars.

No matter how you find your inner garden, remember that it's an ongoing project—gather your prun-
ing shears and fertilizers, because you can continue to
design it.

At the close of *The Secret Garden*, when the
troubled and sickly souls have all been healed, the garden appears as "a wilderness of autumn gold and purple
and violet blue and flaming scarlet." The growth of the
garden and the characters' growth are inextricably en-
twined. There's the beauty: if we tend well to our own
inner gardens, our lives will blossom.

JOURNEY 11

a key

In oneself lies the whole world and if you know how to look and learn, the door's there and the key is in your hand. Nobody on earth can give you either the key or the door to open, except yourself.

—J. Krishnamurti

I am sitting in a motel overlooking the ocean at Cannon Beach, Oregon. In front of me, on a Formica table, lies a room key with a large blue plastic triangle attached to it. I have traveled to this place to meet a group of new friends, but my innate need for solitude has led me to a quiet morning alone. And there, for me, is the key. Alone. A place of no distraction. Here I can hear my own voice, the beating of my heart, the call that pulls me forward.

How often in the last year have I lost this particular key? My days are filled with people—students, colleagues, friends—with lunches and dinners and movies. When I was younger I pulled away more, lost myself in the solitude of creating characters, preparing for a performance, wandering alone in the city I called my home. But these days I find I resist the quiet times, afraid that if I leave my connection to the outside world, I will never find my way back again.

But the key is in front of me. I pick it up, feel its shape and weight against my palm. And instantly I know where to insert it. Into my heart it slides. A door swings open to a staircase leading down. I know I must descend.

Each of us knows somewhere in the depths of our being what the key looks like, and each of us knows what that key unlocks. But much of the time, perverse creatures that we are, we live our lives as if the key

didn't exist. The thing we most need and desire is the thing we resist most strongly.

Isabelle, now sixty, had given up a successful career as a concert violinist when her children were born. She sold her violin when she was thirty-three and never looked back. On her journey she found a small key that she recognized instantly—the key to her old violin case. She quickly found the case, unlocked it, and picked up her beloved instrument. As she began to play, the music flooded into her system, filling her with a joy she thought she had lost forever.

You don't need to know consciously what is waiting to be unlocked. In fact, chances are it will come as a surprise. But there will likely be a deep sense of recognition as well, and maybe even relief. Trust that whatever comes is a message from your unconscious, and let yourself play with the adventure of it. It's like hunting for buried treasure in your own backyard.

A KEY MEDITATION

Now that you're relaxed, I want you to begin to set off on a journey. You can head in a direction you've headed before, or maybe you'd like to travel somewhere new. Maybe you're walking, maybe you're riding, maybe you're flying on a magic carpet. But however you're traveling, be sure to notice what's underneath you. Is there

sand? Earth? Concrete? Notice what's on either side of you as you travel. Are you passing villages or cities, fields or mountains? Maybe you're passing the ocean. Just notice and keep on moving. Notice what time of day it is. Notice the temperature. Notice how the air feels on your skin. Be aware of smells. Listen for sounds. What sounds can you hear close by? Are there birds? The crunch of gravel under your feet? City noises? What sounds are in the distance? Listen carefully. Open your ears. Be specific.

In a moment, somewhere on your path, you're going to find a key. It may be that you have to look for it. It might be on the path in front of you, or it might be off to the side. Maybe it's up in the tree-tops. Perhaps a creature will have to show you where that key is. But however you find it, you're going to find it now. And when you're ready, I want you to pick it up. Hold it in your hand. What's that key made of? Is it metal? Is it glass? Is it wood or plastic? How large is it? What does it feel like in your hand? Smooth? Rough? Warm? Cool?

Maybe it's a key you recognize. Maybe you've never seen it before. But whatever it is, I want you to begin to look around and see what this key opens. You may have to search. You may know right away. When you've found what this key opens, take a moment to observe. Notice how you're feeling. When you're ready, I want you to insert the key and turn it. Letting it open what has been locked until now. If it's a door or a gateway, step inside. Perhaps it's a box or a journal. Open it and see what's in there for you.

Maybe it's something metaphoric. Allow yourself to have that experience. Explore. See what's there for you.

You have entered a place that until now has not been available to you. Why? Why have you been able to open it now? Be curious. Use all your senses. And when you're ready, you can begin to write.

What sort of key did you find? Maybe it was made of iron, wood, or brass. Was it large or tiny? Familiar or not? Perhaps you knew instantly what the key unlocked, perhaps you had to journey further to find where it fit.

In the middle of her meditation, Kendra gasped and began to cry. Then the tears subsided into laughter. The key she found was made of crystal, and without any hesitation, she had inserted it into her belly. That was the gasp. The key traveled deep into her womb, and she remembered the baby she had hoped to have, but had never manifested. The memory was sharp and painful, but she trusted it was a gift and let the key open her

womb. There she found a healthy, happy child. It gave her so much joy to play with that baby. "I'm only forty-one," she announced to the group. "I guess there's still hope—and if not, I'll adopt!"

Timothy, who came to me because of a crippling bout of writer's block that had derailed his novel, found a key to an old wooden box. Inside was a stack of letters that belonged to his grandmother. Reading the letters gave him insight into his main character, and the realization that he needed to use more of his own personal history to move the story forward.

As a symbol of those parts of our psyches that are "locked away" from consciousness, the key appears in stories as far in tone from each other as *Alice in Wonderland* and *Jane Eyre*. It is an archetypal image that underlies the structure of myths and fairy tales and, as such, holds a deep and powerful place in our literary history.

Keys come in all shapes and sizes. Sometimes they unlock an enormous piece of the puzzle, sometimes they just offer a glimpse into an unexamined place. But wherever your key provided entry, know that there is one more piece of your own puzzle that is now open and available to you.

author's note

The journeys included here are offered as a guide, a structure to follow until you are comfortable with traveling your own inner pathways. It is my hope that as your practice deepens you will develop your own journeys, using the process to discover new creative and personal destinations.

Thanks for sharing this part of your voyage with me. I hope you've enjoyed the ride.

MAIA DANZIGER
Los Angeles, California

the author

MAIA DANZIGER is an Emmy Award-winning actress who
has appeared extensively on and off-Broadway, on tele-

vision, and in film. A founder
and former Artistic Director of
The Actor's Company Theatre
in New York, she now lives in
Los Angeles, where she teaches
Relax & Write classes; she also
leads workshops and seminars
all over the world.

To contact Maia regarding workshops or coaching,
please go to:
www.relaxandwrite.com

Made in the USA
Middletown, DE
12 August 2021

45878785R00073